George Washington

Jennifer Strand

abdopublishing.com

Published by Abdo Zoom™, PO Box 398166, Minneapolis, Minnesota 55439. Copyright © 2017 by Abdo Consulting Group, Inc. International copyrights reserved in all countries. No part of this book may be reproduced in any form without written permission from the publisher. Abdo Zoom™ is a trademark and logo of Abdo Consulting Group, Inc.

Printed in the United States of America, North Mankato, Minnesota
072016
092016

THIS BOOK CONTAINS RECYCLED MATERIALS

Cover Photo: Christie's Images/Corbis
Interior Photos: Christie's Images/Corbis, 1; iStockphoto, 4–5; Gilbert Stuart/Detroit Publishing Co./Library of Congress, 5; Zach Frank/Shutterstock Images, 6; North Wind Picture Archives, 7; Photo 12/UIG/Getty Images, 8; Fine Art Images/Heritage Images/Getty Images, 10; Everett Historical/Shutterstock Images, 10–11; Universal History Archive/Universal Images Group/Getty Images, 12–13, 18–19; GraphicaArtis/Getty Images, 15; Francis G. Mayer/Corbis/VCG/Getty Images, 16; Edward Savage/Library of Congress, 19

Editor: Brienna Rossiter
Series Designer: Madeline Berger
Art Direction: Dorothy Toth

Publisher's Cataloging-in-Publication Data
Names: Strand, Jennifer, author.
Title: George Washington / by Jennifer Strand.
Description: Minneapolis, MN : Abdo Zoom, [2017] | Series: Legendary leaders | Includes bibliographical references and index.
Identifiers: LCCN 2016941384 | ISBN 9781680792379 (lib. bdg.) | ISBN 9781680794052 (ebook) | 9781680794946 (Read-to-me ebook)
Subjects: LCSH: Washington, George, 1732-1799--Juvenile literature. | Presidents--United States--Biography--Juvenile literature. | Generals--United States--Biography--Juvenile literature. | United States--History--Revolution, 1775-1783--Juvenile literature.
Classification: DDC 973.4/1092 [B]--dc23
LC record available at http://lccn.loc.gov/2016941384

Table of Contents

Introduction 4

Early Life 6

Leader 10

President 14

Legacy 18

Quick Stats 20

Key Dates 21

Glossary 22

Booklinks 23

Index 24

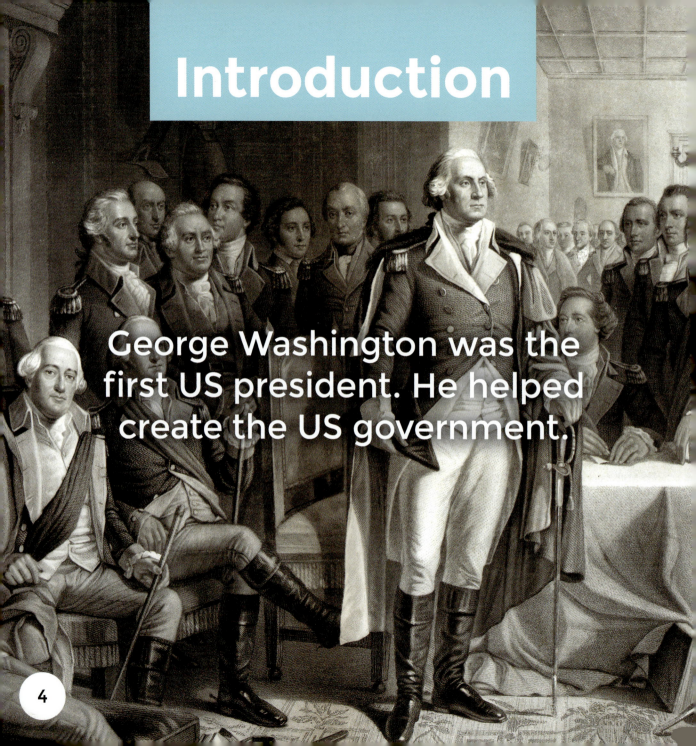

Introduction

George Washington was the first US president. He helped create the US government.

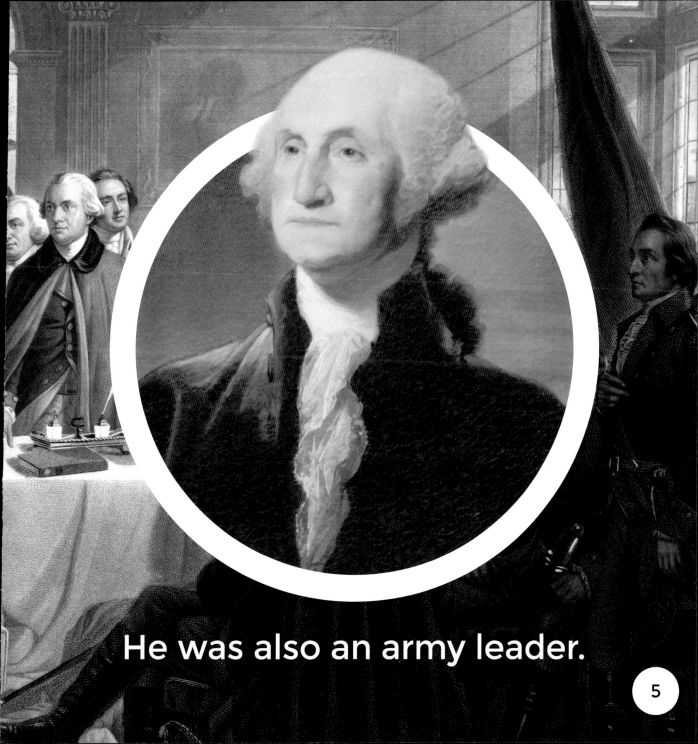

He was also an army leader.

Early Life

George was born on February 22, 1732. He lived in Virginia.

George grew up on a farm.
He learned to survey land.

George fought in a war.

He became an army leader.
He was a **lawmaker**, too.
At this time Britain ruled the American **colonies**.

Leader

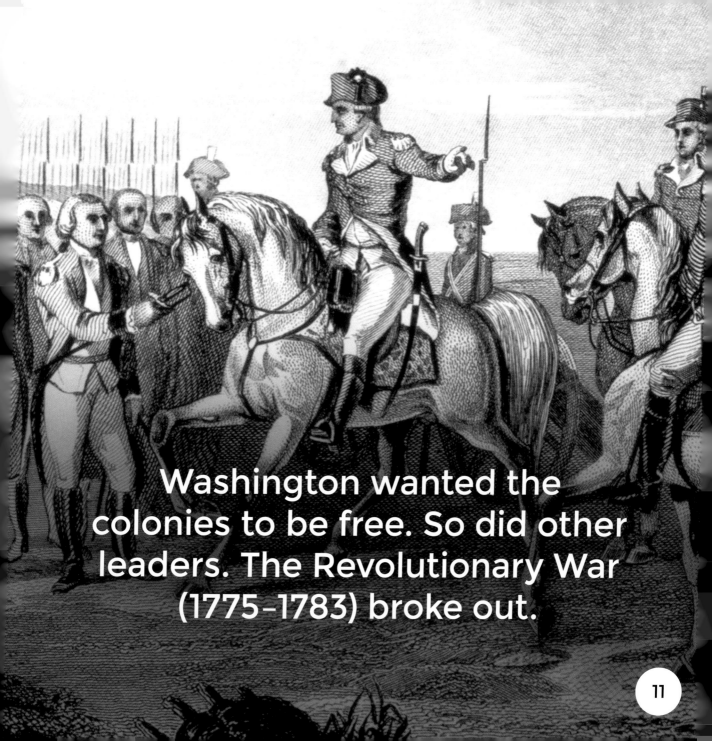

Washington wanted the colonies to be free. So did other leaders. The Revolutionary War (1775–1783) broke out.

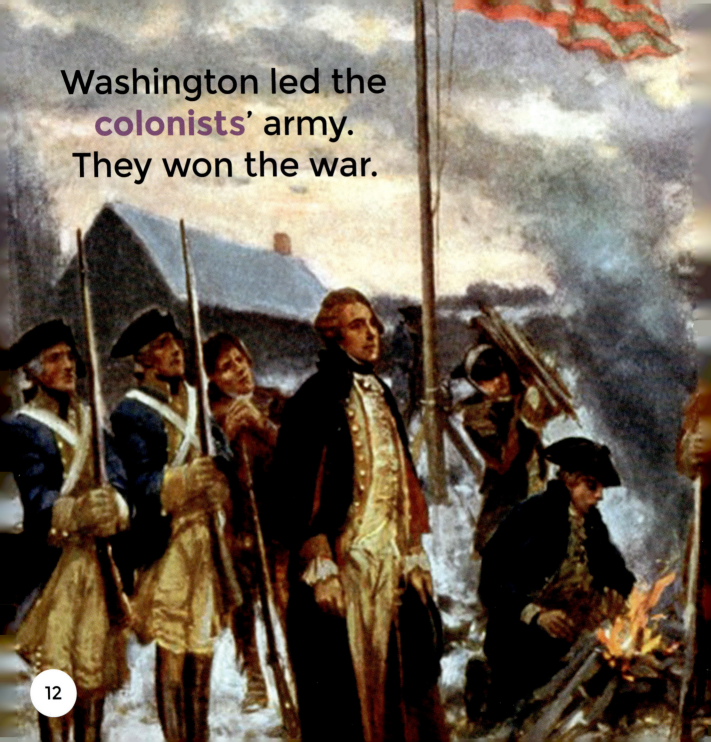

Washington led the colonists' army. They won the war.

The United States became a new country.

President

Washington helped write the **Constitution**. In 1789 he became the first US president.

Washington helped make courts and banks.

He made a plan for the government's spending. He also helped the new country have peace.

Legacy

Washington was president until 1797. On December 14, 1799, he died.

He is often called the father of the United States.

George Washington

Born: February 22, 1732

Birthplace: Pope's Creek, Virginia

Known For: Washington was the first US president. He also led the colonial army during the Revolutionary War.

Died: December 14, 1799

Key Dates

1732: George Washington is born on February 22.

1774: Washington is part of the First Continental Congress.

1775–1783: The Revolutionary War is fought.

1776: The Declaration of Independence is signed on July 4.

1789–1797: Washington is the first US president.

1799: Washington dies on December 14.

Glossary

colonist - a person who lives on land that belongs to a faraway country.

colony - land that belongs to and is ruled by a faraway country.

Constitution - the most basic laws that govern the United States.

lawmaker - a person who makes laws.

survey - to measure an area of land in order to make a map or plan.

Booklinks

For more information on **George Washington**, please visit booklinks.abdopublishing.com

Zoom In on Biographies!

Learn even more with the Abdo Zoom Biographies database. Check out **abdozoom.com** for more information.

Index

army, 5, 9, 12

born, 6

Britain, 9

colonies, 9, 11

Constitution, 14

died, 18

government, 4, 17

president, 4, 14, 18

Revolutionary War, 11

United States, 13, 19

Virginia, 6